Philadelp....u
Travel Guide 2023
for Women

A Captivating Travel Guide for
Adventurous Women: Explore
Philadelphia's Historic Landmarks,
Hidden Gems, and Vibrant Culture

ROLAND RICHARD

Table of Contents

Introduction

Philadelphia invites women from all walks of life to set out on a transformative journey in a city bursting with history, culture, and limitless opportunities. The goal of this guidebook is to inspire women to explore Philadelphia like never before and to celebrate the spirit of exploration.

Philadelphia has a long history of being hailed as a city of firsts, a location where women have forever changed the course of history, the arts, the sciences, and society. Philadelphia's female past is reflected in its streets and sites, waiting to be discovered by the intrepid traveler. It includes pioneering suffragettes, innovative artists, daring campaigners, and trailblazing scientists.

You will embark on a trip that goes beyond the typical tourist experience as you read through the chapters of this guide. You will tour the areas that give Philadelphia its distinct personality, from the Old City's historic district to Fishtown and Northern Liberties' hipster quarters.

You'll stroll around the halls of prestigious museums and galleries, unearthing hidden creative gems and honoring the achievements of women artists who have defied expectations. You will take your taste buds on a culinary journey while enjoying traditional cheesesteaks and farm-to-table treats that highlight the city's culinary prowess.

Additionally, you will become fully immersed in the historical places and iconic locations that have created the identity of the country, fostering a profound respect for the women who were essential allies in the struggle for freedom and justice.

This book is a celebration of womanhood, sisterhood, and the endless possibilities that open up when women embrace the spirit of adventure, rather than just a map of the attractions in Philadelphia. It is an invitation to uncover your inner strength and resilience, to connect with amazing communities, and to pursue your own passions.

Philadelphia welcomes you with open arms, whether you are a solitary traveler looking for empowerment, a group of friends wanting to create lifelong memories, or a woman hoping to rediscover her own sense of adventure. It is a city that begs you to explore it, to become enthralled by its cultural diversity, and to depart with a heart full of inspiration and a soul nourished by the experiences that lie ahead.

So buckle up, pique your curiosity, and get ready for a life-changing adventure through Philadelphia's streets. Together, we will explore the city's hidden beauties, honor the strength of women, and forge lifelong memories.

This is a woman's travel guide to Philadelphia, a city that never ceases to astonish and where the spirit of sisterhood mingles with the lively energy. Let's get started with this memorable tour of Philadelphia's hidden gems.

Chapter 1

Unveiling Philadelphia's Feminine Legacy

You will find a rich tapestry created by the great women who have made an imprint on Philadelphia's history as you explore the city's center. Their tales, which span the spectrum from trailblazers and activists to artists and scientists, should be honored and shared.

Finding Notable Women in Philadelphia's Past At the National Constitution Center, where I first learned about Lucretia Mott's significant contributions as a bold Quaker abolitionist and women's rights campaigner, I first encountered Philadelphia's feminine legacy. I gazed in wonder at her painting and was moved by her unceasing attempts to defy social expectations and pursue justice. Knowing that Mott played a crucial part in setting up the inaugural Women's Rights Convention in 1848 served as a poignant reminder of the willpower and tenacity of Philadelphia's trailblazing women.

As I traveled on, I stopped at the venerable Philadelphia Museum of Art, where I was engrossed in Selma Burke's sculptures and feminist advocacy. Her mesmerizing sculptures, each one a tribute to the beauty and fortitude of women, were all over the museum's corridors. Burke's artistic expression reflected her commitment to social justice and equality, as evidenced by her ground-breaking work on the

Franklin D. Roosevelt profile on the dime and her moving portrait of Booker T. Washington.

Examining the Roles of Women in Art, Science, and Society

A visit to the Franklin Institute, where I was enthralled by the tale of physicist Chien-Shiung Wu, was one of the highlights of my exploration. She gained the moniker "the First Lady of Physics" thanks to her ground-breaking work in nuclear physics and her crucial contribution to refuting the concept of conservation of parity.

As I stood in front of her painting, I was overcome with awe for both her perseverance in a sector that was dominated by men and her unrelenting dedication to advancing scientific understanding. As I traveled on, I came upon

Philadelphia's thriving contemporary art scene, where daring female artists are defying expectations and changing the face of the arts. When I went to galleries in Fishtown and Northern Liberties, I was astounded by the many viewpoints and compelling stories that were presented.

These artists are addressing social concerns and igniting relevant debates with their creative works, which range from provocative installations to brash and emotive paintings. The legacy of women in Philadelphia extends beyond the fields of the arts and sciences. The history of the city is also closely linked to the pioneering women who have significantly impacted social action, education, and medicine.

I learned about the lives of unsung women who fought for social equality, education, and suffrage as I strolled through the historic district. Their unshakable commitment and fortitude served as evidence of the influence that women's voices can have on society. I was reminded of the significant contribution that women have made to forming Philadelphia's history and culture through my personal experiences and first-hand encounters with the city's feminine legacy.

We are continually reminded of these exceptional women's ongoing influence and are motivated to celebrate their accomplishments by the sculptures, murals, and other landmarks erected in their honor. Philadelphia is more than simply a tourist destination; it's a place where you can immerse yourself in the lives and legacies of remarkable women. It motivates us to create our own mark on the world while inviting us to consider the challenges and victories of those who came before us. We pay tribute to the history of these exceptional women and open the door for future generations of powerful women by embracing the spirit of exploration and discovering Philadelphia's hidden gems.

So let's start this inspiring journey together, exploring Philadelphia's hidden gems, honoring the women who have influenced its history, and embracing the spirit of adventure that lies ahead of us at every step. Prepare to be immersed in a city that hums with feminine energy, where the past and present are intertwined, and where the remarkable tales of women are brought to life.

You are cordially invited to explore, learn about, and be inspired by Philadelphia.

Chapter 2

Navigating Philadelphia's Neighborhoods

Philadelphia is known for its dynamic, diverse neighborhoods, each of which has its own distinct personality and attractions. This chapter will go deeper into some of Philadelphia's most alluring neighborhoods and give you a complete road map for traversing these thriving communities.

Old City's Allure: A Historic Haven

With its constrained cobblestone alleyways and admirably preserved colonial architecture, Old City serves as a witness to Philadelphia's extensive history. You'll have the impression that you've been transported back in time to the country's beginnings as you stroll through this area. As you pass by famous sites like Independence Hall and the Liberty Bell, you can feel the area's historic significance.

Exploring the Museum of the American Revolution is a must-do when in Old City. You can immerse yourself in this location's interactive displays and artifacts to learn about the founding fathers' heroic struggles to preserve American independence. The museum offers a fascinating tour through the Revolutionary War, giving visitors a clearer appreciation of the challenges and victories that helped shape the country.

In addition to its historical value, Old City has a thriving artist community. There are many art galleries in the area, presenting a variety of artistic genres and media. Every art aficionado will find something to attract them, whether they prefer modern or traditional pieces. In addition, the area's theaters present enthralling productions, from modest independent companies to Broadway-caliber productions. A few places where you can see a noteworthy performance include the Painted Bride Art Center and the Arden Theatre Company.

You can engage in the exciting nightlife that Old City has to offer after spending time learning about history and culture. The area is well-known for its upscale gastropubs, speakeasies, and bars. Old City's thriving nightlife culture has something for every taste, whether you're looking to sip creative cocktails, try local breweries, or enjoy wonderful cuisine.

Center City: A Fusion of Culture and Urban Energy

Philadelphia's Center City is the city's pulsating center and offers a wide variety of cultural attractions, top-notch cuisine, and great retail opportunities. Philadelphia's famous LOVE statue, which can be found in Love Park, is located in the area. This well-known landmark captures the atmosphere of the city and is a favorite location for both locals and tourists to take striking pictures.

The Philadelphia Museum of Art, which has a sizable collection spanning numerous eras and artistic movements, will please art fans. The museum gives a thorough tour of the world of art, from Renaissance masterpieces to modern works. Don't forget to ascend the famous "Rocky Steps" to take in the city's sweeping views.

A trip to South Street is essential for anyone looking for a distinctive shopping experience. This colorful stretch is a treasure trove for fashionistas and those looking for one-of-a-kind items, known for its varied mix of boutiques, vintage shops, and offbeat retailers. After a day of shopping, unwind at one of the popular eateries and cafés in the area, which provide a wide variety of cuisines to satiate any need.

Another must-see place in Center City is **Rittenhouse Square**. This affluent area is home to opulent boutiques, top-tier department stores, and elegant restaurants. The square itself offers a gorgeous location for a leisurely stroll or a quiet picnic, acting as a tranquil oasis amidst the bustle of the city.

Hip and Trendy Hideaways: Fishtown and Northern Liberties

Fishtown and Northern Liberties, which were once industrial areas, have seen a remarkable transition to become hip and trendy havens for creatives, musicians, and young professionals. These communities have a mix of bright and creative energy, culinary delights, vibrant music venues, and artistic appeal.

Modern art in the city is centered around **Fishtown**. There are various galleries here that display a wide variety of artwork, from modern paintings and sculptures to avant-garde installations. The area also has a thriving music culture, with small clubs showcasing both national and international performers. There is a sound to suit every musical preference, from indie rock to experimental jazz.

Fishtown's neighboring Northern Liberties offer a blend of the old and the new. A distinctive architectural fusion is created when new apartment complexes are built next to historic row houses. Boutique stores, lively eateries, and specialty coffee shops dominate the streets. The Piazza at Schmidt's is a well-liked gathering place where festivals of art and farmers' markets are held. Creativity and involvement in the community are always permeating the air.

Both Fishtown and Northern Liberties have developed into gastronomic hotspots with a plethora of cutting-edge and fashionable restaurants. These communities provide a wide variety of dining alternatives, from farm-to-table restaurants to foreign fusion food. Exploring the always-changing culinary scene, where skilled chefs play with flavors and display their culinary skills, will be a treat for food lovers.

West Philadelphia: Supporting Creativity and Diversity

West Philadelphia is a district renowned for its cultural diversity, rich educational institutions, and thriving arts community. This region, which is home to Drexel University and the University of Pennsylvania, is vibrant with youth, intellectual curiosity, and cultural diversity.

A trip to West Philadelphia wouldn't be complete without visiting these esteemed universities' stunning campuses. The campus of the University of Pennsylvania boasts a blend of modern and old structures, making for an eye-catching setting. Fans of history and anthropology should not miss the University of Pennsylvania Museum of Archaeology and Anthropology, usually referred to as the Penn Museum.

A fascinating look into different civilizations and cultures is offered by the museum's enormous collection of ancient artifacts from throughout the globe.

Modern art and culture are also well represented in West Philadelphia. On the campus of the University of Pennsylvania, the Institute of Contemporary Art hosts exhibitions of cutting-edge and well-known artists' work that provoke thought. A variety of cultural events, such as music festivals, theatrical productions, and book readings, are also held in the neighborhood.

The cuisine available in the neighborhood reflects the community's diversity. You may sample a variety of international cuisines along Baltimore Avenue, including Middle Eastern, Caribbean, and Ethiopian. Due to the gastronomic variety, you can sample the world's delicacies by starting a culinary adventure.

A Culinary and Cultural Journey Through South Philadelphia

The dynamic and culturally diverse neighborhood of South Philadelphia has long been praised for its close-knit neighborhoods, delectable cuisine, and enduring customs. Visitors can explore the fusion of several cultures in this area and savor a variety of delectable foods for a completely immersive experience.

The Italian Market, which enchants visitors with its vibrant atmosphere, fresh vegetables, and genuine Italian delicacies, is the beating heart and soul of **South Philadelphia**. Explore the various stores that offer an alluring range of cheeses, meats, and pastries as you stroll along the lively streets and breathe in the aroma of freshly made coffee. Enjoy a traditional cheesesteak or explore other Italian specialties like cannoli and fresh spaghetti.

However, South Philadelphia's gastronomic options go beyond Italian food. The neighborhood offers a variety of international cuisines that reflect the influence of different groups. The cuisine options in South Philadelphia are as diverse as the residents of this area, ranging from traditional soul food to Mexican street food and Vietnamese pho.

South Philadelphia not only has delicious food but also a vibrant cultural scene. A must-see attraction is Isaiah Zagar's Magic Gardens.

attraction, see. In addition to showcasing Zagar's own artistic vision, this immersive mosaic art setting is a monument to the strength of both community and individual expression.

The Sports Complex, home to the city's top sports teams, puts sports fans right in the middle of the action. A live sporting event or concert at one of the top venues, such as Lincoln Financial Field or the Wells Fargo Center, is an experience that perfectly encapsulates the fire and enthusiasm of the community.

Philadelphia's neighborhoods are an adventure in and of themselves, providing a window into the city's illustrious past, diverse culture, and thriving culinary scene. Each Philadelphia neighborhood has its own distinct charm and treasures just waiting to be discovered, whether you're exploring the historic charm of Old City, engrossing yourself in the bustling urban excitement of Center City, or learning about the hidden gems of Fishtown, Northern Liberties, West Philadelphia, and South Philadelphia. So put on your walking shoes, take a detour, and let Philadelphia's fascinating neighborhoods take you on a memorable journey.

Chapter 3

Memorable Galleries and Museums

Philadelphia is a city that values art in all of its manifestations, from classics to cutting-edge modern works. I'll take you on a tour of some of the city's most fascinating galleries and museums in this chapter, where you can immerse yourself in the world of art and be inspired by the amazing collections they hold.

Masterpieces and More at the Philadelphia Museum of Art

The Philadelphia Museum of Art is a cultural landmark perched majestically at the end of the Benjamin Franklin Parkway. A stunning vista of the city skyline will welcome you as you make your way up the fabled "Rocky Steps" to the building's great entryway.

A universe of artistic marvels is waiting inside. The museum's extensive collection spans millennia and features works from many different artistic movements and cultural backgrounds. There is plenty to enthrall any art aficionado, from Impressionist classics to modern installations, from European Renaissance paintings to ancient Egyptian treasures.

The Philadelphia Museum of Art's collection of American art, which displays the various artistic expressions that have defined the country, is one of its attractions. This collection chronicles the development of American art, from the classic works of Thomas Eakins and Winslow Homer to provocative modern pieces.

The museum also features a diverse schedule of temporary exhibitions that explore a range of subjects, historical eras, and aesthetic movements. These special shows provide a novel viewpoint and the opportunity to learn about new artists and artistic narratives. At the Philadelphia Museum of Art, there is always something intriguing going on, from major exhibitions to specialized ones.

Exploring Women's Art at the Pennsylvania Academy of the Fine Arts

In addition to being a renowned art school, the Pennsylvania Academy of the Fine Arts (PAFA) also has a museum that honors the achievements of women artists. It is the oldest art museum and school in the country and was founded in 1805. It has been instrumental in fostering and advancing women's artistic talent.

Famous female artists like Mary Cassatt, Cecilia Beaux, and Violet Oakley, among others, have pieces in the museum's collection. The art world has been forever changed by these artists' breaking down of barriers and defiance of social standards. The PAFA offers a venue for showcasing their abilities and paying tribute to their legacies.

The Pennsylvania Academy of the Fine Arts also conducts exhibitions that are exclusively centered on women artists and their artistic journeys in addition to its permanent collection. These exhibitions provide a forum for discussion and an opportunity to recognize the contributions that women have made to the field of art by giving insight into their distinctive viewpoints and stories.

The Barnes Foundation's Inspirational Exhibitions

An absolute gem in Philadelphia's art scene is The Barnes Foundation. It was established by Dr. Albert C. Barnes in 1922 and now holds a world-class collection of early Modernist, Post-Impressionist, and Impressionist works of art. The collection's layout is original and thought-provoking, blending the lines between many aesthetic traditions and resulting in unexpected contrasts.

The galleries of the Barnes Foundation are brimming with works of art by painters including Renoir, Cézanne, Matisse, and Picasso. Additionally to the diverse array of artistic expression on display, the collection includes ornamental arts, pottery from Native American tribes, and African art.

The foundation puts on a number of fascinating exhibitions that explore many facets of art history and present novel viewpoints and motivational stories. These exhibitions offer a greater knowledge of the artists and their creative processes while showcasing the range and depth of the collection.

The Barnes Foundation offers educational programs, seminars, and workshops in addition to its collection and exhibitions, giving art lovers of all ages the chance to interact with art more deeply. There are many ways to discover and appreciate the art within these revered halls, from guided tours to interactive activities.

Philadelphia's museums and galleries are a voyage of inspiration and discovery. These organizations open doors to new worlds of creativity, providing a glimpse into the minds and visions of artists throughout history.

From the masterpieces housed in the Philadelphia Museum of Art to the celebration of women's art at the Pennsylvania Academy of the Fine Arts and the captivating exhibitions at the Barnes Foundation. As you embark on an extraordinary exploration of Philadelphia's museums and galleries, get ready to be enthralled, informed, and moved.

Chapter 4

Enjoy Your Taste Buds: Food and Drink Experiences

Philadelphia is known for having a thriving culinary scene where a wide range of flavors and culinary customs come together to create a heaven for food lovers. In this chapter, we cordially encourage you to experience the city's exquisite cuisine, from traditional dishes to farm-to-table specialties, and to learn about the artisan breweries, distilleries, and wineries that help Philadelphia become a center of beverage excellence.

Dining Delights: Farm-to-Table Delights and Iconic Cheesesteaks

Without indulging in the cheesesteak, Philadelphia's most recognizable dish, no gastronomic tour of the city would be complete. These delectable sandwiches, which feature melted cheese, sauteed onions, and thinly sliced beef, are a Philadelphia staple. For any food connoisseur, a trip to South Philadelphia's Pat's King of Steaks and Geno's Steaks, where these delectable delicacies have been served for decades, is a must.

The culinary culture in Philadelphia, however, goes much beyond cheesesteaks. The farm-to-table movement is growing in the city, and many eateries are committed to using local ingredients and showcasing regional cuisines. These restaurants provide a culinary experience that is not only excellent but also supports regional farmers and encourages sustainability. They provide everything from seasonal food to meats that have been farmed sustainably.

Philadelphia is home to a wide variety of award-winning restaurants run by renowned chefs for those looking for a great dining experience. These restaurants push the frontiers of gastronomy and provide a feast for the senses with creative tasting menus and culinary fusion experiments. Philadelphia's culinary scene has something to suit every palate, whether you're in the mood for French food, Asian fusion, or contemporary American meals.

Craft Breweries, Distilleries, and Wineries: The Local Scene

Philadelphia has developed into a center for craft alcoholic beverages such as beer, spirits, and wine. There are many breweries in the city that create distinctive and excellent beers, and the craft beer scene is flourishing. You may experience a wide range of craft beers at prominent breweries, including Yards Brewing Company, Dock Street Brewery, and Evil Genius Beer Company, from silky stouts to zesty IPAs.

Philadelphia also has a growing craft distillery culture in addition to beer. Local distilleries use both tried-and-true procedures and cutting-edge processes to create a variety of spirits, including whiskey, gin, vodka, and rum. Visitors can learn about the distillation process and enjoy the distinctive flavors of spirits manufactured in Philadelphia by visiting distilleries like New

Liberty Distillery and Manatawny Still Works, which provide tours and tastings.

Wine lovers in Philadelphia will also have plenty of company. Despite not having large vineyards, the city has a thriving wine culture with many urban wineries and wine bars. These businesses create a wide range of wines using grapes from different geographical areas, both domestically and abroad. Whatever type of wine you prefer—reds, whites, or sparkling—Philadelphia's wine scene is a singular opportunity to taste and discover various wine genres.

Philadelphia is renowned for its vibrant cocktail culture in addition to its craft breweries, distilleries, and wineries. Numerous bars and speakeasies can be found throughout the city.

where talented mixologists create one-of-a-kind drinks utilizing fresh ingredients from the area and creative taste combinations. Philadelphia's cocktail culture is likely to please even the most discriminating cocktail lovers, with everything from traditional cocktails to cutting-edge mixology marvels.

Indulging your palate in Philadelphia involves more than just satiating your hunger and filling your thirst; it also involves becoming a part of a culinary and beverage scene that values originality, excellence, and regional flavors.

Philadelphia provides a mouthwatering variety of culinary experiences that will leave you wanting more, from famous cheesesteaks to farm-to-table delights and craft breweries to urban wineries. So be ready for a delicious excursion through the gastronomic and libation riches of the city and get your mouth primed.

Chapter 5

Historic Sites and Iconic Places

Philadelphia is a historically rich city where you can still hear the echoes of the past in the streets and landmarks. In this chapter, we urge you to explore the city's prominent locations and immerse yourself in the stories of independence, revolution, and intrigue as you dive into its rich historical tapestry.

Where Freedom Began: Independence Hall and the Liberty Bell

The Liberty Bell and Independence Hall, the very icons of American freedom and democracy, must be seen during any trip to Philadelphia. The Liberty Bell, which is kept in the Liberty Bell

Center, has stood as a constant reminder of the fight for liberty and equality. The structure's well-known crack serves as a reminder of the tenacity and perseverance of the American people. You cannot help but feel awe and admiration for the ideas it represents as you stand in front of this famous treasure.

Independence Hall, where the Declaration of Independence and the United States Constitution were discussed and enacted, is located next to the Liberty Bell. This revered structure serves as a monument to the founding ideals and the emergence of a nation. You can follow in the footsteps of the founding fathers and become fully immersed in the historical events that transpired inside Independence Hall by taking a guided tour of the building.

These important sites serve as reminders of the ongoing fight for freedom and equality as well as providing a window into the formation of a nation. They encourage visitors to ponder the values that support American democracy and to think about their own contributions to upholding and furthering those ideals.

Investigating Revolutionary Women at the American Revolution Museum

Although men's efforts during the American Revolution are well recognized, stories of women who played important roles are frequently ignored. By highlighting the outstanding women who influenced history, the Museum of the

American Revolution aims to address this. From nurses to spies, political activists to spies, and camp followers to nurses, these women bucked social norms and left a lasting impression on the struggle for independence.

The museum brings to life the tales of women like Abigail Adams, Deborah Sampson, and Molly Pitcher through interactive exhibits, immersive displays, and thought-provoking narratives. It demonstrates their valor, tenacity, and unflinching commitment to the cause of freedom. A deeper grasp of the Revolution's complexity and a greater appreciation for the hidden histories that influenced the country can be gained by perusing the displays on Revolutionary women.

The Museum of the American Revolution serves as a potent reminder that people from all areas of life, including women, whose achievements are just as essential and deserving of acknowledgment, have also played an important role in shaping history.

A Hauntingly Fascinating Experience at Eastern State Penitentiary

A voyage into the past can be experienced by visiting Eastern State Penitentiary, where the crumbling walls still carry the ghosts of those who were imprisoned. Eastern State Penitentiary, formerly the most renowned and expensive jail in the world, is now a hauntingly beautiful ruin that draws tourists in with its Gothic style and ominous aura.

You can't help but feel both fascinated and uneasy as you stroll through the empty cell blocks. Innovative solitary confinement practices at the penitentiary serve as a vivid reminder of the terrible realities of the past while also fostering thought and repentance. Stories of infamous criminals and daring escapes are set against the somber backdrop of the crumbling cells and corridors.

Eastern State Penitentiary is a place for introspection and contemplation in addition to its creepy attraction. Visitors are challenged to contemplate the moral ramifications of incarceration and the need for prison reform through informative tours and sobering exhibitions. It serves as a reminder that history is not only found in books but also permeates the actual places we live.

Philadelphia's historical sites and prominent locations are a journey through time that provide a window into the people and events that helped shape the country. Each location has significance and offers a tale that encourages thought, meditation, and a deeper comprehension of the nuanced layers of American history, from the revered halls of Independence Hall to the eerie hallways of Eastern State Penitentiary. So go forth and let these famous historical sites and landmarks lead you on a fascinating journey through history.

Chapter 6

Unleash Your Style: Shopping and Fashion

Philadelphia is a bustling center for retail and fashion, in addition to being a city rich in history and culture. We welcome you to release your sense of style and go on a shopping expedition around the city's distinctive shopping districts in this chapter. You'll find boutique gems, regional designers, and handcrafted craftsmanship that will up your fashion ante.

Philadelphia's Unique Shopping Enclaves: Boutique Treasures

Philadelphia is home to numerous quaint and unique neighborhoods that provide a wonderful selection of boutique shopping opportunities. **Rittenhouse Square**, a neighborhood in Center City, is one such enclave. This upmarket area is teeming with high-end boutiques and designer shops that offer a carefully curated collection of current clothing, accessories, and home furnishings. Rittenhouse Square offers individuals looking for rare and chic fashion finds a wide range of options, from well-known luxury companies to independent designers.

Visit the **South Street area** for a more bohemian and varied retail experience. This thriving area is well recognized for its independent merchants, vintage shops, and specialty boutiques. You can find unique apparel items, oddball accessories, and artistic works that capture the character of the area here. A person with an adventurous and unconventional sense of style should visit South Street.

The Old City district, where history and style converge, is another must-see retail district. There are a variety of chic boutiques, art galleries, and design stores in this attractive neighborhood. Here, you may browse a wide selection of clothing options, from modern and cutting-edge styles to classic and vintage-inspired items. The medieval buildings and cobblestone streets of Old City add a special character to your shopping experience.

Learning about regional designers and artisanal craftsmanship

Local designers and craftspeople in Philadelphia are a thriving community that puts their passion and creativity into what they do. You may find distinctive designs, support local artists, and buy one-of-a-kind items that express your distinctive style by investigating the city's fashion scene.

The Philadelphia Fashion Incubator is one of the best places to find regional designers. This creative center, which is located in Center City, supports up-and-coming designers by giving them a venue to display their creations. The Fashion Incubator provides a curated collection of apparel, jewelry, and accessories made by up-and-coming designers, enabling you to stay on top of fashion trends while promoting regional business.

Pay a visit to the **Philadelphia Art Alliance** if you want to learn more about the realm of handmade crafting. This cultural landmark promotes and exhibits the creations of regional artisans, such as jewelers, textile designers, and leatherworkers. Here, you can find stunning handmade items that combine age-old methods with cutting-edge design principles. You can buy one-of-a-kind, exquisitely crafted goods at the Philadelphia Art Alliance while also helping to preserve traditional artisanal techniques.

Philadelphia offers a variety of purchasing possibilities to meet various budgets when it comes to price estimation. Prices for designer goods and luxury brands may be higher in upmarket retail districts like Rittenhouse Square. However, there are also more reasonably priced fashion options available in the city, particularly in areas like **South Street and Old City**, where independent boutiques and vintage shops provide distinctive and reasonably priced bargains.

Philadelphia is a fashionista's and style-seeker's dream come true. The city's shopping districts cater to a variety of interests and inclinations, from the boutique treasures in Rittenhouse Square to the bohemian charm of South Street and the blend of history and style in Old City.

Finding regional designers and craftspeople gives your wardrobe choices a unique flair and enables you to contribute to Philadelphia's thriving creative scene. So, let your personal style shine through and go on a shopping excursion that celebrates your uniqueness while showcasing the city's distinctive fashion options.

Chapter 7

Outdoor Adventures and Parks

Philadelphia may be a busy city, but it also has a ton of gardens, parks, and other green areas that provide a haven from the city's bustle. We welcome you to immerse yourself in the splendor of nature and discover the outdoor getaways Philadelphia has to offer in this chapter. These outdoor sanctuaries offer the ideal setting for rest, renewal, and connection with nature, from the vast Fairmount Park to the charming Longwood Gardens and the tranquil Rittenhouse Square and Washington Square.

Trails, picnics, and serenity at Fairmount Park: Embracing Nature

Over 2,000 acres and a variety of outdoor recreation activities may be found in **Fairmount Park**, one of the biggest urban park systems in the United States. Fairmount Park offers a calm haven inside the city limits with its rich vegetation, scenic streams, and winding trails. The park's large path network is ideal for all types of outdoor exercise, whether you want to take a leisurely stroll, jog, or ride a picturesque bicycle.

Fairmount Park is home to a number of historic landmarks, including the well-known Philadelphia Museum of Art and the lovely Japanese House and Garden, in addition to its outdoor entertainment options. These historical sites and the park's natural splendor merge together in a special way, fusing art, history, and nature. Gather your picnic supplies, look for a shaded area beneath a tree, and enter the tranquility of Fairmount Park to take in a leisurely meal amidst the views and sounds of nature.

A Floral Paradise: Longwood Gardens Exploration

Longwood Gardens, a horticultural wonderland just outside of Philadelphia, promises to be a feast for the senses. This renowned botanical garden, which spans more than 1,000 acres, is home to an extraordinary collection of plants, expertly tended gardens, and breathtaking examples of horticultural craftsmanship.

A stunning variety of hues, aromas, and textures will greet you as you stroll along the flower-lined pathways and explore the numerous themed gardens. The magnificent conservatory at Longwood Gardens is recognized for housing a wide variety of plants from all over the world. Step inside and let yourself be carried away by vivid floral displays, desert vistas, and tropical rainforests that will leave you in awe of nature's beauties. Each conservatory offers a distinctive botanical experience, from the imposing Orchid House to the luxuriant Palm House.

Longwood Gardens, in addition to its magnificent plant collections, also hosts seasonal activities such as extravagant fountain performances, outdoor concerts, and holiday light displays. These unique activities add to the gardens' enchanted ambiance and provide guests with lifelong memories all year long.

Relaxing Strolls in Rittenhouse Square and Washington Square

Rittenhouse Square and Washington Square are urban outdoor retreats that provide solace in the middle of the metropolis. Rittenhouse Square, a beautifully manicured park with tree-lined walkways, lush lawns, and attractive fountains, is found in the affluent Rittenhouse area.

It is a popular gathering spot for both locals and tourists, providing a tranquil environment for barbecues, leisurely walks, or just taking in the scenery. The area is a bustling and dynamic attraction since it is flanked by charming cafes, chic stores, and art galleries.

The historic **Society Hill neighborhood's Washington Square** is home to a tranquil atmosphere with a rich history. This charming park has a stunning central fountain, seating under trees, and historical markers. You'll travel back in time as you stroll through Washington Square because the area is filled with tales and recollections from the city's past. The serene backdrop of the park makes it the perfect place for introspection, relaxation, and thought.

Philadelphia's parks, gardens, and outdoor getaways provide a haven from the rush of the city. These outdoor havens offer a connection to nature, tranquility, and opportunities for renewal.

You can choose to explore the vast trails of Fairmount Park, lose yourself in the floral paradise of Longwood Gardens, or take a leisurely stroll through Rittenhouse Square or Washington Square. So put on your walking shoes, take a deep breath of the fresh air, and allow Philadelphia's outdoor places' natural beauty to uplift your spirit.

Chapter 8

Wellness and Self-Care: Renew Your Mind, Body, and Soul

It's critical to prioritize our well-being and schedule time for self-care in our hectic, demanding lives. For people looking to refresh their brains, treat their bodies, and feed their souls, Philadelphia has a wide range of possibilities. The yoga studios, wellness facilities, and spa retreats in the city will be covered in this chapter as places to find seclusion, relaxation, and holistic renewal.

Find Your Zen at Yoga Studios and Wellness Centers.

Yoga fans will find plenty of yoga studios and wellness facilities in Philadelphia, making it a refuge for them. To promote your physical and mental well-being, these facilities provide a variety of yoga courses, meditation sessions, and holistic wellness activities.

Yoga on the **Ridge**, a top-notch yoga studio in Philadelphia, is situated in the tranquil Roxborough district. All levels of practitioners can find a welcoming atmosphere at Yoga on the Ridge. No matter if you are a seasoned yogi or a beginner, knowledgeable instructors will lead you through vinyasa, hatha, and restorative yoga.

You can perform soft yin poses that encourage relaxation and deep stretching or energizing flow sequences to increase strength and flexibility. You can start on a journey of self-discovery, emotional calm, and physical energy at Yoga on the Ridge in a supportive and safe environment.

Philadelphia is also home to wellness facilities that treat health holistically. In the thriving Fishtown district, **The Healing Arts Collective** provides an integrative approach to wellbeing by fusing techniques like acupuncture, massage therapy, and energy healing.

This center encourages balance, healing, and general wellness with a focus on the mind-body-spirit link. You can benefit from therapeutic massages to relieve stress and tension, try acupuncture to reestablish energetic flow, or investigate energy healing techniques to balance your body's natural energy systems. The Healing

Arts Collective offers a thorough and revolutionary method of self-care.

Pamper Yourself and Rejuvenate at Spa retreats.

Philadelphia's spa retreats provide a place for unwinding, relaxing, and rejuvenation when it comes to indulging in opulent self-care treatments. These retreats offer a haven where you may unwind from the stresses of everyday life and indulge in therapies that sooth your body, revive your mind, and stimulate your senses.

The **Rittenhouse Spa & Club**, situated in the posh Rittenhouse Square district, is a well-known spa resort. This well-known spa provides a variety of superb services delivered by knowledgeable therapists in a serene and opulent setting. Every service is intended to improve your wellbeing, from reviving facials using premium skincare products to tension-relieving massages catered to your individual requirements. As the concerns of the outer world fade away and you set out on a pleasant voyage of self-care and renewal, give yourself over to the healing touch of skilled hands.

The Logan Spa, located inside the city's exquisite and cutting-edge luxury enterprise, The Logan Hotel, is another notable spa retreat in Philadelphia. An oasis of calm is offered by the Logan Spa, where you may rest, refuel, and relax. Choose from a selection of decadent services, including specialized massages that target your tension points, reviving body wraps that nourish and purify, or manicures and pedicures that will make you feel pampered from head to toe. The Logan Spa is a haven of peace where you can prioritize self-care and restore your inner and outer beauty with a focus on customized attention and great service.

The cost of wellness and self-care experiences might differ in Philadelphia depending on the type of service and the location. **Yoga sessions typically cost $15 to $25 per session**, giving people of all financial backgrounds an affordable option. Depending on the length and type of treatment, wellness center services like **acupuncture or massage therapy typically cost between $80 and $150 per session.** Spa services have a wider price range, with entry-level therapies starting at roughly $100 and more expensive services like all-day spa packages It is It

It is usually essential to confirm prices, special offers, and package packages with the relevant studio, facility, or spa.

Philadelphia offers a wide range of health and self-care alternatives that invite you to refresh your body, mind, and spirit. Philadelphia offers a haven for self-care, relaxation, and holistic well-being, whether you want to discover your zen through yoga and meditation in one of the city's warm studios or indulge in soothing treatments at an opulent spa resort. Therefore, seize the chance to give your health top priority and let Philadelphia be your entryway to rebirth and rejuvenation.

Chapter 9

Celebrating Womanhood: Events and Gatherings

Through a diverse selection of festivals, conferences, and other meetings focused on women, Philadelphia is a city that embraces and appreciates them. These gatherings offer beneficial chances for networking, individual development, and the building of caring communities.

Women-Centric Festivals and Conferences

Philadelphia holds a number of annual conferences and festivals that highlight the contributions, abilities, and voices of women. The

Women's Film Festival, which usually takes place in the spring, promotes conversations about women's representation in the film industry while showcasing the works of brilliant female filmmakers. Depending on the occasion, admission to movie screenings and panel discussions often costs $15 to $25.

Women working in the technology industry get together at the Women in Tech Summit, which is held in the fall. Women can connect, educate themselves, and be inspired by one another at this conference, which offers captivating keynote speakers, engaging seminars, and networking opportunities. Depending on early-bird discounts and package choices, the Women in Tech

Summit's registration costs typically vary from $200 to $400.

Networking Possibilities and Empowering Communities

Philadelphia offers a wide range of networking opportunities and empowers communities all through the year. **Women Owned Law**, a networking organization for female attorneys, holds frequent gatherings where its members can interact, exchange ideas, and work together. The cost of going to these networking events varies, with typical ticket costs falling between $20 and $50.

The Women's Business Development Center (WBDC) offers information and continuing assistance to female business owners. The WBDC hosts networking events, conferences, and seminars all year to assist women in starting and expanding their businesses. Depending on the event, attendance at WBDC events can cost nothing or a small donation of $10 to $30.

These gatherings offer worthwhile chances to interact, gain knowledge, and develop among welcoming groups.

Finally, Philadelphia's festivals, conferences, and networking opportunities for women provide enlightening opportunities for women to connect, celebrate their accomplishments, and support one another. Women have specific dates to put on their calendars, such as the Women's Film Festival in the spring and the Women in Tech Summit in the fall.

Throughout the year, Women Owned Law and the Women's Business Development Center offer networking events. Depending on the particular event and its features, different events have different attendance fees. Women can broaden their networks, get fresh viewpoints, and cultivate deep relationships within supportive groups by taking part in these events. These gatherings give women the confidence to embrace their femininity, celebrate their accomplishments, and work together to achieve even more.

Conclusion

Motivating Thoughts and Further Research

Take a minute to think back on the amazing experiences you had and the significant impact this city had on your travels as you come to the end of this travel guide for women to Philadelphia. You have been thoroughly introduced to Philadelphia's rich history, vibrant neighborhoods, engaging museums, culinary pleasures, historic sites, empowering events, and much more throughout the chapters.

Philadelphia has embraced your curiosity and praised your sense of adventure, welcoming you with wide arms. You have been surrounded by the tales of extraordinary women who have changed this city's history and made contributions to its art, science, and society ever since you first set foot here. You have been motivated and given power by their legacies, which have served as a reminder of your own inner fortitude, resiliency, and ingenuity.

You've been able to explore Philadelphia's various neighborhoods and learn about their individual charms and characteristics. You have wandered through Old City, a historic sanctuary where the past and present are intertwined. You have been drawn to Center City by its cultural attractions and the exciting energy of city life.

With their hip and creative hangouts, Fishtown and Northern Liberties have captured your attention and given you a taste of the thriving artistic scene in the city. West Philadelphia has welcomed you with its inventiveness and diversity, inviting you to explore its varied medley of communities and cultures. You have started a culinary and cultural trip in South Philadelphia by delighting in the tastes and customs that make up this melting pot.

Philadelphia's museums and galleries have sparked your creativity and extended your horizons. You have been mesmerized by the masterpieces on display at the Philadelphia Museum of Art, which have taken you to various times and places while showing the brilliance of artists throughout history.

You have learned about the works of women artists who have made a lasting impression on the art world at the Pennsylvania Academy of the Fine Arts, and you have been inspired by their creativity and vision to pursue your own goals.

You now have a greater understanding of the transformational effect of art thanks to the Barnes Foundation's exhibitions, which have stretched your thinking and provided food for thought.

It has been a pleasure treating your taste buds to Philadelphia's diverse food and beverage scene. You have started a culinary journey unlike any other, from relishing the renowned cheesesteaks that characterize the city's culinary reputation to indulging in farm-to-table treats that highlight the fresh vegetables of the area.

You've learned about the rich beverage culture of the city by visiting the neighborhood artisan breweries, distilleries, and wineries, where you may sample handcrafted drinks that capture Philadelphia's creative spirit.

You now have a better knowledge of Philadelphia's significant place in American history as a result of your investigation of the city's historical sites and iconic locations. You have been reminded of the importance of freedom and democracy by Independence Hall and the Liberty Bell.

Women's contributions to determining the fate of the nation have been honored at the Museum of the American Revolution, inspiring you with their bravery and tenacity. The horrific events at

Eastern State Penitentiary have spurred reflection on the complex facets of human history as well as the importance of compassion and justice.

As you reach your destination, pause to thank the several people and organizations that contributed to the creation of this guide. Your journey through Philadelphia has been instructive and enlightening thanks to the dedication of the scholars, historians, artists, and writers.

Your trip to Philadelphia has been a transforming and empowering one, to sum it up. As a woman tourist, the city has welcomed you and given you the opportunity to discover its hidden treasures, engage with its thriving neighborhoods, and honor the historical accomplishments of women. May the memories and inspirations you've gathered as you say goodbye to this guide inspire you to embrace the limitless opportunities that lie ahead in the City of Brotherly Love.

Printed in Great Britain
by Amazon

24948244R00050